AF497772

If Words Could Hold You

MA.C.A

TABLE OF CONTENTS

TABLE OF CONTENTS

TABLE OF CONTENTS

TABLE OF CONTENTS

TABLE OF CONTENTS

*Another spill of thoughts,
another melody of emotions.*

Wanderer

I can tell everyone

that *I am lost,*

and wait until someone

offers me the map.

But that's not the way

life goes.

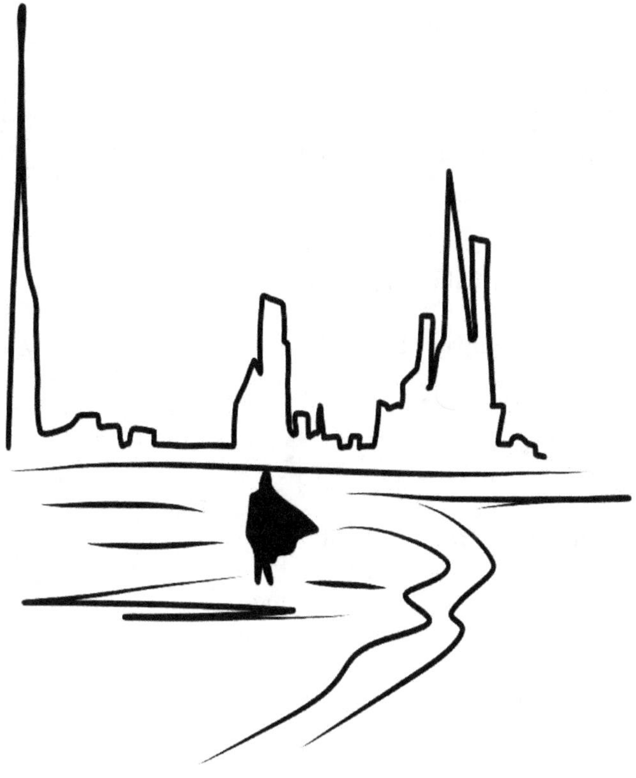

Right Way

How can I follow *my heart*

when my feet buckle

every time I feel it breaking?

How can I follow *my mind,*

when I'm always lost

in overthinking?

And maybe it was just right to go

wherever *my soul* is leading me.

Optimistic Side

I always

tried to look

on the *brighter side* of things,

no matter how hard it was to see,

no matter how cloudy the sky

seemed to be,

and no matter how far *happiness*

is away from me.

Stuck in Time

Everything was *too much,*

but *not enough* at the same time.

It seemed like everything

was *overflowing,*

yet all I ever did

was to watch it

as it got *closer* to me.

Unsaid

I was lost in *my own mind,*

too many times.

And I don't know what's better.

To keep in *silence* after getting hurt

or hear other people's sentiments

they've been *hiding* for a very long time.

Because both of them

hold so many thoughts

that remained to be unsaid.

Half Empty

I can't choose the *feelings*

I want to have,

and I don't know

which one is the better.

To feel *nothing*

or to feel *everything*

all at once.

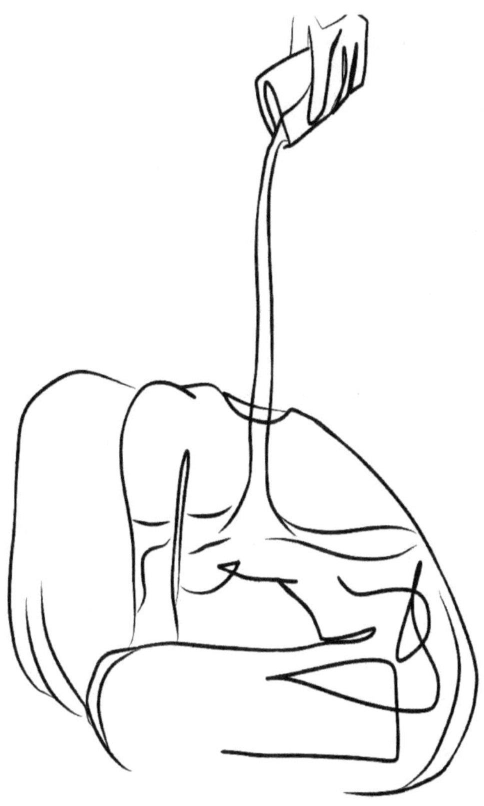

Holding Tighter

Why does *time* remind me

that I need to let *people go,*

when all I want is

to be with them

forever?

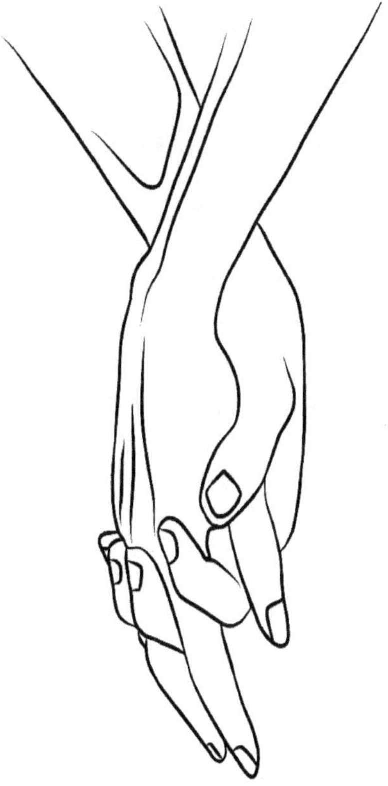

Beginning of an End

But I won't *stop*

writing about us,

even if it means *reliving*

all of the *memories* we've had.

Even if it opens all the *scars*

I thought has already gone

in the *past*.

I Shouldn't be Drowning

Trusting you

was like diving into the water,

not knowing how *deep* it was.

Not having any idea of

what I was going to see

underneath.

But I *believed*

that somehow

you'd let me *breathe.*

Tsunami

Crossing the oceans for you

terrifies me,

because I don't know

how to swim.

And then,

I thought that *loving you*

also terrified me,

but I let it *consume me* anyway.

Suffocation

Maybe I've *held you*

so tight,

that you started to *slip away*

from my grip,

like a pile of sand

escaping from

in between my fingertips.

IF WORDS COULD HOLD YOU

Beautiful Infinite Space

I've imagined

painting *your name*

across the night *sky,*

when there's

no *moon and stars*

but only clouds

to stare at it.

IF WORDS COULD HOLD YOU

One-sided

For some *reasons,*

we may have thought

that we indeed

belong with those people

we loved,

but didn't love us back.

I think that's love.

We love,

not expecting

something in *return.*

Wilted

You used to be

my pink, red, green, blue

and white roses,

combined in a single vase.

But now,

I am a *grassless garden*

without any single flower

growing in it.

Call Me

I love the *way*

you *say* my name.

I love each and every *sound*

that *goes out* of your mouth,

like you're tasting and *treasuring*

every curve and line of it

before you say it out *loud.*

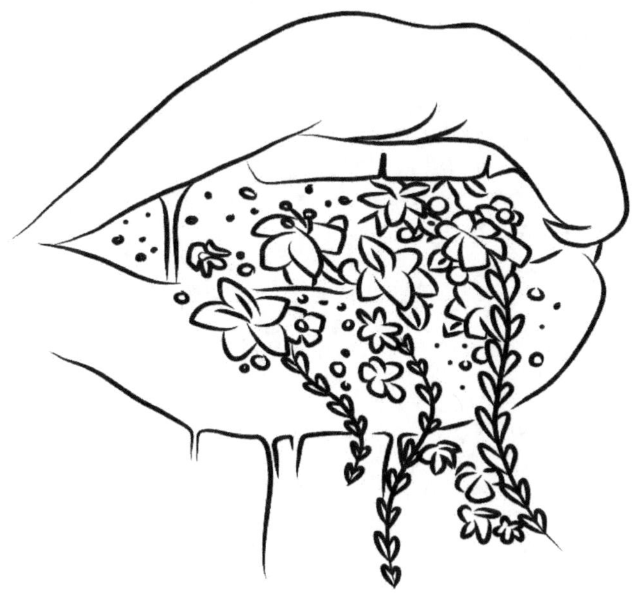

Lacking

I'm *filling* a huge glass

and somehow,

I already felt *empty*

before I reach the half of it.

You see,

I always thought

that I was *never enough*.

And I *wish*

you were never the glass.

One More Glance

I wish I could *live*

among the stars,

so whenever I try

to *look* for you,

I can see *wherever* you are.

And if ever you try

to peer up at the sky,

our *gazes will meet* again

just like the *old times*.

Tell the Universe

I want more than a physical touch,

I want an *open mind*

and an *understanding heart*;

I want more than holding hands,

I want *soul connection* that nothing—

No one can tear apart.

Bilingual

Getting to know you is like

learning a language

that I've never heard before—

it was *confusing* at first,

probably even *frustrating*

every now and then,

yet it was worth it.

It will always be *worth it*

to know you even more.

You Moved On

I saw you *smiling* at her,

as if she gave you the world

you've been *hoping* to have

and for the first time,

I know how it feels

to be *drowned*

even if

I'm out of the ocean.

Parallel Versions of Us

Because I don't want to be

in another *universe*

if you're not going

to be there with me.

I'm aware that I *can't* have you,

but knowing that *you exist*

in the same *world* as mine

becomes the *truth* that still

makes everything fine.

IF WORDS COULD HOLD YOU

Mismatched

Maybe my hands

weren't *meant* to hold yours,

even if my heart *refused*

to let them go.

It's as if a *flower* still appears

and *blooms* in the middle—

in a *crack* of a concrete road.

Last Encounter

I am *stuck* between hoping

that I could *unmet* you,

and wishing that

I could *meet* you a second time,

yet in a *different* situation.

Favorite Star

I saw him being happy

with *someone else,*

and I thought I couldn't stare more,

but then I decided to wait.

I waited for his eyes to *shine*

brighter than the sun,

and when it finally did,

I realized that *it's okay.*

It's alright,

as long as I can see the bright in his eyes,

even if I'm no longer the *reason behind.*

We Became Excerpts

"I'm so scared of leaving you."

These were the words

I always wanted

to hear from you,

a six-word story,

and a *million thoughts*

of what we could be.

First Heartache

I was once *scared*

of not being able to find

a love we've shared.

That no matter

how many *miles*

I *walk* through,

the wind will always

lead me *back* to you.

Think About Me

And I'll always *wonder* about

what's going on your mind,

what's *burning* in your heart,

but I'll always be terrified

of not being able

to find my name

written inside

any of them.

IF WORDS COULD HOLD YOU

It Could Have Been You and Me

And it was one

of the *hardest decisions* I made—

to walk away from someone

I knew I can always *fight* for.

Yet the truth is that

love was always hard if it's *one-sided,*

even if it's exactly

what you *thought* you're looking for.

Oxygen

Of course,

I can live *without* you,

but please *remember*

that there was

a *moment* in my life

when you made me feel

like I *couldn't*.

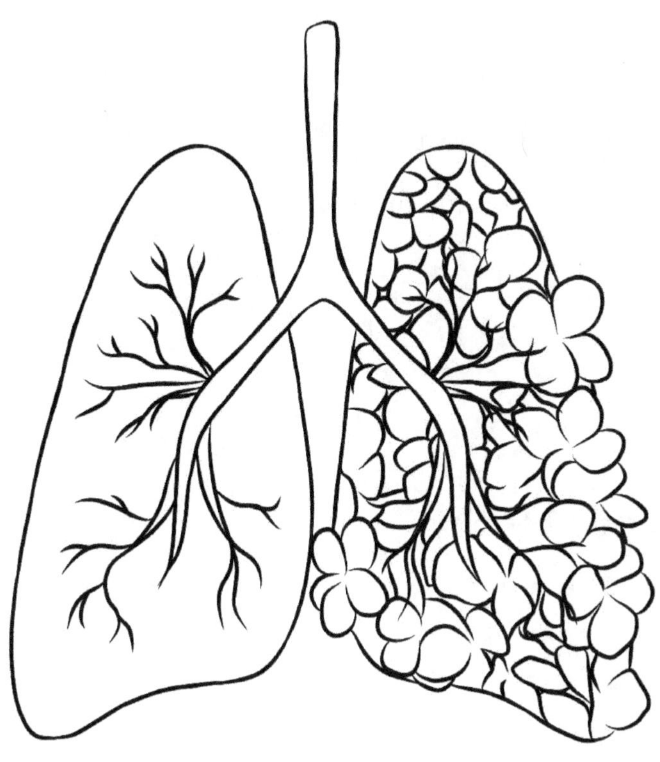

Whole

You *deserve* someone

who wouldn't turn around

and run away from you

once they've seen your *flaws*.

You deserve to be loved

wholeheartedly,

even for the things

you seem to *hate*

about yourself.

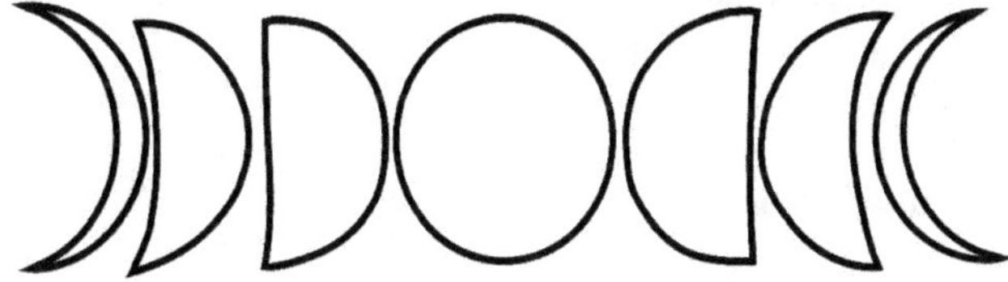

Phases And Feelings

I hope you'll find someone

who will love you,

no matter what *mood* you're in,

as much as how

you *still* love the moon,

even if it *shows* you

just *half* of its *beauty*.

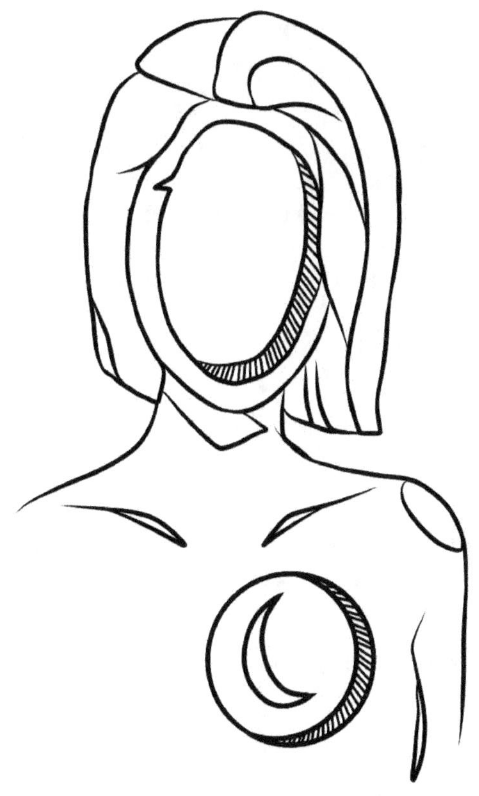

Someday, It Will be Our Time

And when there's no more

tears left to fall,

please raise your head up high

and remember that

we're still staring

at the *same wide sky.*

You and I—

both hoping

that everything *will be fine,*

even if sometimes

our stars refuse to shine.

Blooming

Please *take care* of yourself,

not because *no one* else will

but for the reason that love

should *start* from deep within—

that somewhere

inside you

it must begin.

Tomorrow

Darling we will *cry*

with our hands on our knees.

We will close our eyes

with *tired souls*

and *dreamless* sleeps,

but I always hope that

one morning,

we will wake up

with *courage*

and *wonderful* beginnings.

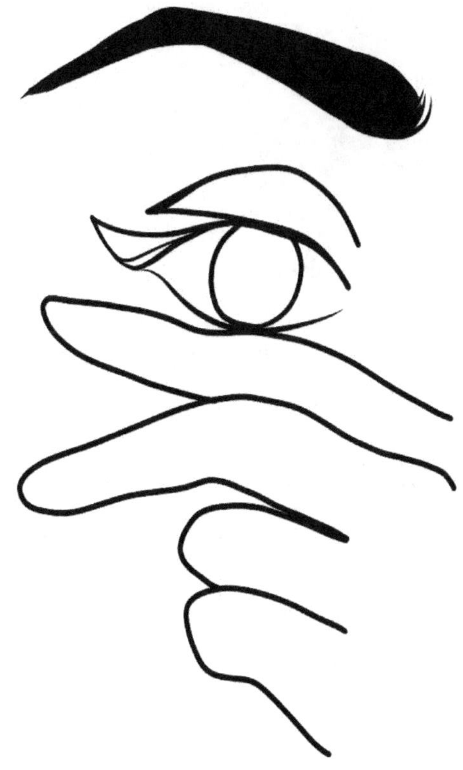

Hope isn't a Myth

I'll always look up

just to see how beautiful

the *full moon* is,

even if it hurts my neck,

even if I couldn't find

any reason to do it.

May you always find

beauty in everything.

May your heart *rise*

even if it falls

time and time *again*.

Pushing Down Blockages

I hope that someday,

you will be *brave* enough

to *break* the barriers

that have been keeping you

away from your *dreams*.

I hope that someday,

you will be *strong* enough

to fight for

your *own* happiness.

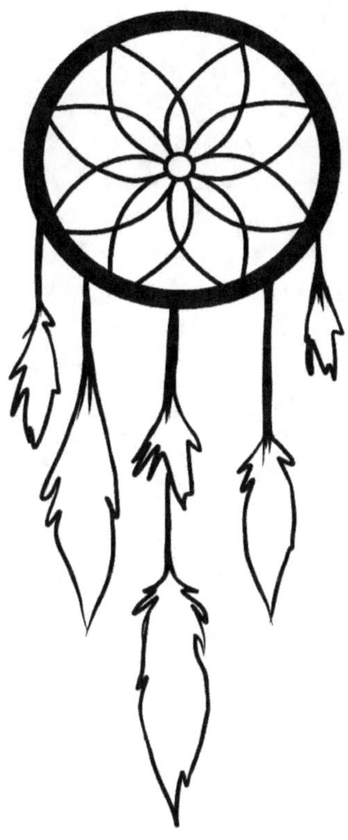

Filtered

Not everyone you meet

will *understand* you,

Not everything you see

should *concern* you,

And not every word you hear is *true*.

Because if you let it go inside you,

everything might *destroy* you.

We Need More Proofs

I hope that you'll always have

enough courage to *tell the truth*—

To hear it

and to *accept* it,

even if it doesn't look

as *stunning* as

every *single lie*

in this world.

Perfect Imperfections

It's okay to make *mistakes*

from time to time,

as long as you're *learning* from it.

Because you also need

to make some room

for *improvements,*

for you to build

the *best version* of yourself.

Fly Free

Take a *deep breath*, darling.

Remember that

there are some things

you just *need* to let go,

no matter how *strong*

you refuse to.

Night and Day

The sky gets *darker*

for you to see the stars

and somehow,

if life ever gets *gloomy*,

I hope you'll find

where *happiness*

could be seen.

Light Up

Just like the sun,

you will shine *naturally*,

no matter how many times

the *storm* would try

to *dim* your light

and *destroy* everything

that you could be.

Progress

You can be stronger than

who you were *yesterday* —

as much as you want,

as long as

you *never* let someone

stop you

from doing *better*.

Cleansing

Please know

that cutting *toxic people* off

may also mean

giving yourself the *chance*

to breathe a little deeper

and having enough *space,*

so that you could shine

a little bit *brighter.*

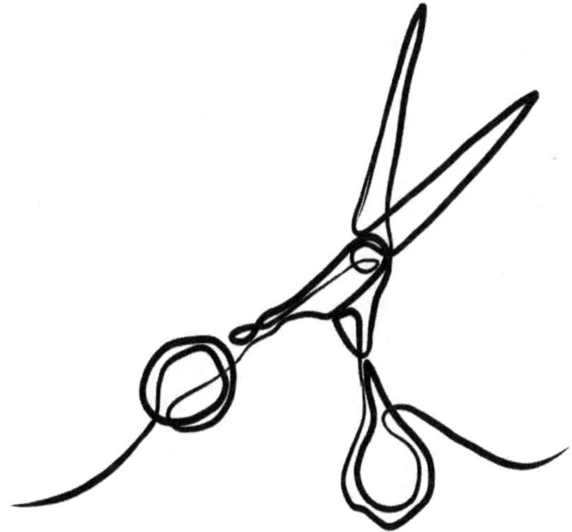

Kindness from a Wild Heart

She builds

an *empire* of flowers

that bloom inside *her heart,*

and picks out and leaves

every piece of it

wherever place she goes

and whoever

person she meets.

IF WORDS COULD HOLD YOU

Just Another Page

Not all *endings* happen

with waving hands

and loudest of *goodbyes,*

because sometimes endings

were made of *teary eyes*

and the *saddest* of smiles.

If I Were Me

One of the saddest things

in this strange world

is *watching* the person you love

crying over *someone else,*

and all they wanted you to do

is to just *listen,*

while they tell you the reason

why their heart is *breaking.*

Silent Echo

And sometimes

we *shout* the things

we *never* want to say,

and *whisper* to ourselves

all the things

our hearts

want to hear.

Love May Mean a Lot of Things

And some people

will ask you

to *dance* in the rain,

while others

will *walk* with you

under their umbrellas.

And some people

will *show* you

how to do *both*.

Transparent

Opening up yourself to someone

is one of the *bravest* things

you could ever do.

Because it's never easy

to be *vulnerable,*

when all you ever wanted was

to build the *strongest wall* —

all around you.

"I should have said more," she said.

"I should have said everything—
not to everyone else
but most especially to myself."

Solitary Life

I love solitude.

Not because I hate people but because that means I'm aware of my own existence. That I know I'm still alive and surviving the difficulties of life. I love it because somehow, I've realized that sometimes when no one else is making you feel wanted, you need to explore things on your own. There's no need for anyone to remind you that you're worthless.

I know that no one truly survives alone, but sometimes life gives you challenges that you need to overcome mostly on your own.

A Glimpse of the Past

If I'm given a chance to turn back time and change something, I won't even change anything.

I would just take the opportunity to turn back time when I experienced the happiest moment in my life.

I would just watch how I laughed with people I was happy to be with.

I would just watch my face looking up at the beautiful sky. I would just watch how I stared at the little kids on the street. I would just watch how I slept at the public bus. I would just watch how I smiled at people I treasured the most. I would just watch the happy version of me, the person I used to be.

That's what I would do.

To see myself in someone's perspective.

To take a glance at the person I loved the most but I used to care the least. I don't want to have more regrets.

All I want is to take a glimpse of the past and go on in life, as I should be.

Never Been a Fairytale

There's a kid in me that will always believe in happy endings.

A little girl—who always looks up to her prince charming.

But darling, there's also an old soul within me that seems to live in her own reality.

Someone who always expects things to change.

Someone who always tries to understand why people leave and why some things need to end.

They Call it Adulting

And as much as I hate to say it, I just realized that as I grow older, I already accepted that some people will not always be there for me every time I need them.

That no matter how wide I open my door, they would never come in. That no matter how loud I shout their names, they wouldn't turn around and face me. I already accepted the fact that they also have their own problems. That sometimes they need to save themselves first.

They weren't being a bad friend nor a selfish one. But it was just us, human beings wanting and searching for a mean to survive.

And yes, I understand— even if it broke my heart not only once but too many times.

Bet We Want to Live

I could smile after a day of heartbreak. I could laugh while sadness is trying to creep inside my head. I could continue walking even if it means going into the darkness.

I could do something that would change my life. I could choose between different options, even if I know that some of them don't really exist.

Life is a game that I might not win. But I realized winning isn't the main reason anymore.

It's about trying, learning, and growing—which all go along with failing.

What's Bad Inside

And if ever I'd become the toxic person that I'm scared to be, I'm really sorry. I'd sincerely apologize for doing the things I thought I would never do.

But please remember, I'm still trying to figure things out.

I'm still learning to become a better version of me.

Take Care, Self

I'm sorry for leaving and hurting people while I was trying to save myself.

But I wouldn't apologize for learning how it's important to have self-love and self-peace more than anything else.

Wishful Thinking

Maybe it would be easier if I could take my heart out of my chest and inspect the broken side. I want to see what part of it needs stitches or needs to be fixed in general.

Maybe it would be easier if I could just fix it in just a second or even for several minutes and hours. And after doing everything to make it look new again, I would put it back inside my chest.

Maybe it would be easier if I could just turn it on and off, so that I could just shut down those feelings I don't want to have. And I could have the chance to keep those pleasant ones forever.

Maybe all of these will make everything easier. But life is more than that.

Not all things are quite easy, and the rest are indeed just harder than what they seem to be.

Brave Little One

I'm proud of my heart for being so small, yet able to handle every single feeling sometimes I don't even know.

And no matter how many times it shattered painfully, the broken pieces pull themselves back together—making it whole, keeping all the things in place and accepting all the feelings, no matter how much they hurt so badly.

Words from Someone You Never Know

This is a love letter for someone who don't know me at all:

I wish I could see how stunningly beautiful you are today. I wish to see you somewhere in an unexpected moment. When we're both slowly walking and treasuring each and everything that surrounds us. I wish to hear how wonderful your day went and what made it even more special. I wish you could tell me all the things that bother your mind.

This is an apologetic letter for someone who don't know me at all:

I'm sorry I couldn't go there to give you a warm hug and tell you that everything is going to be alright. I'm sorry I wasn't able to cross your way and smile at you and tell the corniest joke that can make you laugh so loudly. I'm sorry if my words can't lessen the pain you're feeling right now. I'm sorry that some people don't feel sorry at all for the bad things that they have done to you. I'm sorry if life is hard and the world seems to suffocate you.

This is a gratitude letter for someone who don't know me at all:

Thank you for being there when no one else seemed to be interested in everything I wrote. Thank you for listening to me every time I'd tell you how my day went. Thank you for not giving up on life and for doing everything you can just to reach all of your dreams. Thank you for saying "hi" and "hello". Thank you for asking me if everything's fine and if life's kind to me. Thank you for breathing and existing in this world. I just wanted to say thank you so much for being the light in my darkest times. I'm so thankful that you're still fighting and you're proving that you're brave enough to hold on to life. You're strong enough to keep moving forward.

If I Can't Call You Mine

If people will be named after colors, I'll call you purple. The kind of purple that melts in the sky when the sun is about to set and take a rest for a while. The type of purple that makes my heart jump a little bit and lit up the excitement in my eyes.

If people will be named after flowers, you'll be my rose. That no matter how painful your thorns are, I'll embrace and cage you in a warm tight hug. Even if it makes me bleed red that might tear my heart apart.

If people will be named after seasons, I'll choose summer among all of those four. You'll be the sun that would touch my skin and make my day brighter along the way. You'll make me love the ocean more and dance to groovy songs. You're the season which will never get tired of warming up my heart when winter would try to cool it down with its cold breeze. Making you the favorite season of my life.

If people will be named after places, I'll call you home.

Not Paris, nor New York.

You're the place that will always make my heart lonely when I'm away, because I'll surely miss you the moment that we'd take our separate ways.

You're the shelter that protects my heart, the one I will always run to no matter what I'm feeling. Happy, angry, sad, jolly, grateful, or in love. Because you always understand and know the real me. You've seen me on my ups and downs, and still accepts me for who I am.

I'll name you after a place that doesn't have a fancy name, yet will always be the one that would tell me that it's okay to feel different emotions.

That it's okay to be me.

You will always remain in my heart, no matter where I go.

And because people have identities, and so are things.

But you and your name will always be my favorite.

Unknown Inspirations

I read stories about someone who doesn't know me. Someone who haven't seen me yet. Someone I only considered as imaginary.

I sing the lyrics of the band without them hearing me. A group of talented people who haven't listened to my voice yet.

I admire someone's beauty which I've only stared at a random magazine inside a crowded bookstore. A face with only one expression. A face I've never seen in whole.

And I realized, that it was important how you make a heart dance. How you turn a frown into a smile without forcing it to happen. Because maybe it was one of the best things that we can do.

To turn sadness into happiness without meaning to. That maybe in the end, we can try to replace hate with love, even if we thought we weren't capable of doing it.

Even if we thought that it was just an impossible truth.

You Could Also Be That Someone

I hope you'd meet someone who will understand your every move. Like an audience who loves to see beneath a dancer's step.

Someone who will listen to you even if you're not saying any single word. Like a song lover who still listens to the part where there are no lyrics anymore but only the sound of playing instruments.

I hope you will meet someone who will love you, not only at your brightest days but will love you even more on your darkest days. Someone who will not get tired when they see you at your weakest. Someone who will lift you up and never let you down.

I hope that you will meet someone who inspires you to continue in life.

I hope that someone will prove to you someday that even if you're not perfect, you deserve love more than you've had ever imagined.

Anyone Else

You don't have to be with someone who makes you feel like you need to pretend, to be something you're not.

You deserve more than that.

You deserve to be you, while being loved by someone.

Our Own Fiction

We'll be talking about the galaxies, even if I don't know all of their names. We'll be naming all the stars we'll see while pointing our fingers to the sky.

We'll be staring at the sunset even if people see us standing in one place for several minutes and find us weird.

We'll be laughing at our own jokes after we share some serious stories. We'll be singing rhymes for kids and will be singing brightly like one.

We'll do things people thought we would never do.

The cutest things that tickle our hearts and bring happiness to our souls. Things we always wished we could do from the very beginning.

We'll be happy together genuinely.

We'll write every chapter of our life.

We could be the characters in our own love story, but I want you to know that we could always be our own selves and grow as an individual, together.

And that's what I'd love to do with you.

Human Nature

Love doesn't stop at saying "I love you".

Love doesn't end at telling someone how much you love them.

It starts when you think of them every time you aren't together. Every time you open your eyes in the morning and remember how wonderful your dreams are last night, because you thought of them before you go to sleep.

It doesn't end when two hearts decide to beat as one.

It doesn't stop even if you already said goodbye.

In this world where people think that hate exists too much, love goes on. And it will never end, because this world needs and deserves more love.

Somewhere in Paradise

Sometimes letting go will take you to a place where love isn't the most complicated thing, where true love flows naturally, and where everything is more than just what your eyes can see.

Let Me Sit Beside You

And I hope someday you won't tell me about heartbreaks. You won't tell me how things fall apart. You won't ask me for my advice because you no longer need them.

Instead, you will tell me how wonderful life is. And I won't stop you from describing how it feels to be whole again.

Then how you were able to pick up and put the broken pieces back together. I will be there, smiling at you every time you pause on talking and glance at me.

I will be there, listening. Because that was one of the best stories I would pay attention to.

You're Not Who They Say

Don't let people take away that softness in your heart.

Don't let them change you into a person that doesn't make you feel better.

Some people will try to provoke you to do the things you will regret afterwards. Breathe and calm yourself before doing things that caused by your anger. Forgive those people who say bad things about you, but it's always okay to remember the things they did to you.

Not to bury the hate in your heart, but to understand that there are people who don't have the same kindness like yours. Sweetheart, don't let them dim the light inside that beautiful heart of yours.

Hold On

They say that if you're doing what you love, even if there's no one out there to witness it, you're exactly doing it for yourself. I want you to do that, when you're sad and you feel like the world is sinking like a ship and you're at the bottom of the sea.

When you feel like you can never escape, I want you to do what you love. If you want to shout but couldn't do it without drawing attention to yourself, I want you to write everything that makes you feel sad on a paper. Write them. Every single of it. And when you're done, throw it at the fire and watch it burn until it turns into ashes.

If you love singing but you claim that it doesn't love you back, sing anyway. Sing your favorite songs with all of your heart.

If you love dancing but your feet don't cooperate, dance anyway. Dance until you laugh like crazy and you feel like all the worries have already vanished.

If you love watching movies, watch your favorite movie all over again. Even if you can still remember all the dialogues, watch it anyway.

If you want to walk outside, walk until you find a bench where you can sit. Until you find a place where you can eat. Until you're done staring at the stars, at the lovely sky.

Read your favorite books, and feel its words like the first time. Read it until you fall asleep.

Remember that you should do it for yourself.

Do anything you truly love without hurting yourself.

Just this once, if you're not used on doing it every time.

I want you to do something that will help you to breathe deeply and freely and feel life at its finest.

I want you to shine because you're doing what you love.

I want you to be so bright, that you can no longer see the things behind the darkness.

Even for once, I want you to defeat the darkness itself.

Courage, Dear

A little girl might keep on telling you that the moon follows her wherever she goes.

She might try to count how many stars are there in the gloomy sky. She might even want to stare at the blaring sun without protecting her precious eyes. She might happily run on the street laughing, without slippers on her feet. She might eat her food giggling not minding staining her dress. She might seat on the swing, swaying, and facing the strong blowing wind. She will tell you that she can do things even if you already told her that she couldn't.

Sometimes a child's determination stays with them forever—

and I hope yours hasn't gone, too.

Rushing Will Trip You

Don't force yourself to understand each and everything immediately.

You can't always solve all of your problems in just a matter of few days.

You can't always run to a place in just a matter of seconds.

You can't sleep and wake up early every day, because sometimes we need more rest than usual.

There are times when people will say things to you but they wouldn't explain it any further, even if you ask them many questions.

Some things were made for waiting and you don't need to rush them. Some things were made to teach you how to be patient and to deal with things slowly. Always remember, just because other people are living way too fast doesn't mean that you need to be faster and be ahead of them.

You will figure out everything sooner or later. Just keep going but take a rest every now and then, especially when you really need to.

Rest, heal, and move forward.

Don't Stop Yourself

When you feel like crying and everything is falling apart, you're allowed to mourn for your feelings and hide in the dark.

When you think that the world is tearing you into tiny pieces, you're allowed to ignore the world and give yourself some time to cope up.

When your heart is being pierced by something you can't explain and you have no idea what else there's left to do, you're allowed to sleep. Take a rest and have wonderful dreams. When you're wounded, you're allowed to drink some medicine and have the time for you to heal.

But when you're done and the bruises are all gone, you're allowed to stand tall and prove to yourself that no matter how things go wrong and so painfully, the sun will always rise and you can step up to another new beginning.

Give Yourself Chance

Sometimes you just have to try.

You just have to pick a pen and write down the things that you've been caging in your mind for years. You just have to open that book and start reading the story of life you've been imagining. You just have to send that message to someone you've been admiring from afar, to thank the people who are always on your side no matter how worst the situation becomes, and to stand up and start walking towards the place that'll bring you the genuine happiness you've been hoping every night.

Sometimes you just have to truly open your eyes and pull yourself away from the monsters that tell you, "No, you can't do it." Try to take even just a single risk, without hurting yourself too much. Try to tell yourself that you can do it. But don't be complacent.

One step at a time.

As they say, big things start at small beginnings.

All you have to do is to try.

Things that Matter

Stand up after falling on the ground. Remember that your dreams will not come after you, and you wouldn't achieve them if you keep running away without even trying.

Speak up, even if you feel like your voice isn't loud enough for the world to hear. When everything you feel will not be pretty like fireworks when they explode at once.

Wake up and go out, not because you want to have fun but because the world is beautiful that it keeps on waiting for you to explore.

Do things, not because you want to impress the people around you but because you want to be a living inspiration to someone who is scared to see all the things that surround them.

Be the human being who lives and feels.

Be someone who isn't afraid to dream, and is not afraid to work hard for it.

Show the best version of you.

Live, love, and inspire.

Come Back Stronger

There's nothing beautiful with heartbreak. There's nothing fine with the feeling that brought you the loneliest and most sleepless night. There's nothing good with those tears you keep on wiping away from your eyes at 3 am when no one is around. Feeling your own heart collapsing and falling piece by piece was never a wonderful thing.

Do you know what's beautiful?

What's fine?

And what's good?

Heartbreak doesn't feel like flying with colorful butterflies, but sometimes it's okay to walk alone and cherish your own company for you to be able to know yourself even more.

It doesn't make you love the morning and the sun, but sometimes it's fine to watch the moon while everyone has gone to sleep. It doesn't look like bright little stars on the night sky, but sometimes instead of hating the rain, you should listen to what it has to say, not with your ears but with your heart and mind.

Heartbreak hurts but it's always up to you if you're going to let it destroy you or make you a stronger person.

When it's about your own heart, you always have a choice.

Unconditional

It's never truly wrong to crave love from someone. No one ever said that it was a mistake to fall in love with someone you know won't feel the same way towards you. They call it unconditional love when you don't expect anything in return.

Selfless.

Brave.

When you accept that feelings sometimes will not be mutual.

Yet I hope that you should be willing to give the same kind of love to yourself.

That even if you did a lot of mistakes, you resist the urge to hate yourself. Instead, I hope that you forgive yourself and learn from the lessons you will meet along the way. Because that needs a lot of patience, kindness, and courage, my dear.

Loving yourself even if the world tells you not to.

Forgiving yourself even if other people say you don't have to.

Being kind to yourself even if you sometimes think you couldn't.

Darling, this is what you should always remember,

especially when you feel like everything around you is like killing every little piece of you.

Don't ever forget that you deserve love, more especially from yourself.

Don't let your light fade away.

Stars are there with a purpose.

And so are you.

Déja Vu

Suddenly, you met someone who told you the same story. Someone who told you about the same path you've walked through. And this time, you truly listened. You looked at them in the eyes while all the memories started coming back from the past.

Suddenly you were like listening to an old song.

You were like seeing an old scene you thought you've already forgotten. You were like in the darkness again. A darkness that was surrounded by the voices you thought will never exist again. You were like watching an old movie, the one you don't want to remember anymore.

You're hearing the same story from a different person.

This time, the tears were not coming from you. It's from someone you haven't known when the same story happened to you. But this time, you know why it has to happen that way. This time, you were different. Because you already learned the lessons behind that story.

And it's time for you to try saying that someone how you overcome all the obstacles you thought you can never get through.

Sun and Moon

Darling, I hope that you'll meet someone who knows what you deserve. From the things you wanted to feel to the words you needed to hear.

I hope you will meet someone who will not mock you nor laugh at you when you start blurting out all the crazy things that touched your heart. Someone who will not walk away from you when you start telling them about all the precious things that run through your mind. I hope you will meet someone who will not only promise you to stay, but also do everything just to keep you with them.

I hope you will meet someone who will embrace every little piece of you. Someone who understands your passion and supports you in loving it.

And if you meet that someone, I hope that there will be mutual feelings between the two of you. That even if you are the moon and he is the sun, both of you will always remember that you always light each other's life. That when you get tired, he will always be there to lift you up and vice versa.

I hope you will find someone who will make you feel all the best things you deserve to experience. Because like other people in this world, you deserve to be genuinely happy, even if you think that you'll never be.

Trivial

If only I could, I would tell you that life was easy.

I would tell you that it's just about the good times and the colorful smiles. That it's just about always waking up in the morning and feeling that everything is alright.

If only I could, I would tell you that bad things don't happen and they are just false nightmares hunting you in your sleep. That there are no such things as lonely souls and broken heart's wings. That there are no worries and stressful days.

If only I could, I would tell you that depression is just a myth. That you shouldn't be scared for you can never have it.

If only I could, I would tell you that everyone will still treat you kindly, even if you've done bad things in your life. That there are no such things as insecurities and jealousy. That there are a lot of people who will still love you, even if you haven't met each one of them.

If only I could, I would tell you that there are no such things as thunderstorms and wild earthquakes that would try to ruin our homes. That a hurricane only wanted to drown us with its love, not with its overflowing hate at us.

You see, if only I could I would only tell you about the beautiful things, but I would be lying for the rest of my life. If I only tell you about these things, you'd surely ask for proof and I would end up with empty hands.

Because I have nothing to give you when life had already showed the truth to you.

Bring Out the Best in You

You'll wake up one day, realizing how tiring life is and hoping for the world to stop spinning and for people to stop talking. Wishing that you're somewhere else but here.

You'll love to be out of this universe and imagine for yourself being in a different place, to be in a different situation.

You'll want to change things and arrange it like your own puzzle, easily solved and built in just for one second. Things will be hard. And the waves will be stronger. You'll wish that you don't have to face it. You'll try to turn around and run away, but you'll realize that you cannot escape this.

That for you to get through it, you'll need to lift yourself and fight it.

And when that day comes, you'll have all the courage you've been hiding in your heart.

You'll find out how brave you are. You'll see what's more than that face, who is always staring back at you in the mirror.

You'll know that you are capable of more. You'll then realize that life won't give you something you can never take. That failure isn't something that should put you down and every success is worth every single tear that has ran out of your eyes.

That you are the strongest person you'll ever know, even if the world tried to make you believe otherwise.

Someday, it'll be all right.

Someday, you'll realize that life is still worth fighting for.

That living a life is still something we should dream of, no matter how ruthless it can be at times.

Maximum Reach

I hope we'll never run out of time.

I hope we'll never say it's too late to chase our dreams and love ourselves in each passing moment.

I hope we'll choose what's best for us, no matter how confusing it might become.

I hope we'll live life to the fullest, so we won't regret anything in the end.

Now

And sometimes, it's okay not to dream about anything.

It's okay to be confused of what you truly want to happen in your future.

Sometimes, it's okay to live through the day, and survive everything that's in the present.

Story Telling

But then there's a time when you are not waiting for an answer. You're not waiting for any reaction from that someone you're trying to talk with. All you ever wanted was to say everything that you feel. To burst out that single bubble you're keeping from a very long time. To release all the weight that's resting on your mind, those heavy things hiding on the curves of your heart.

There's a time that you wanted someone to listen. You wanted them to open their ears, while you tell them about all the stories that are stopping you from moving your feet forward.

You just wanted to tell everything—all of it.

Because sometimes you get tired of giving your time to someone, that you wanted to rest for a while.

Sometimes all you want is someone, even if it will only last for a few minutes. Someone who would sit beside you and genuinely listen to each and every word that you'd say.

Someone who will give their time not to judge you, but to choose silence because they know that you also need it, too.

Seconds, Minutes, and Hours

We have 24 hours a day.

They say you need 8 hours to have a healthy sleep.

That has left you 16 hours to chase your dreams.

But sometimes, we spent half of it doing the happiest things. And when something has gone wrong, our day happened in reverse. That we choose to close our eyes, for more than 16 hours having the sweetest fantasies.

And we will be awake with confused minds for less than 8 hours, yet wishing we can obtain our dreams in just 24 hours.

Ordinary and Special

Some of the days will be like children running, playing, and laughing at the park. Families eating together inside a comfy restaurant. Teenagers walking hand in hand. A lovely lady inside a fancy boutique trying a dress with a smile. Some of the days will be sunny as if the whole world decided to spread a happy vibe.

But we both know, that some of the days will also be like silence in a crowded room. Like a man alone, sitting on a bench watching people pass by in front of him from morning to noon.

Some of the days will make you love yourself more, yet some days will make you realize how people tend to judge one another.

Some of the days will make you feel like you want to change the world because of everything you feel, because of the worst things you've seen.

Some of the days will make you want to smile at every single stranger you meet. As if you want them to see how wonderful the day is.

Some of the days will tell you who you are, and some days will drag you somewhere else, trying to tell you that you're lost again.

Yet maybe, every day might be all the same for you. Because you've been doing the same thing again and again. But when you try to look back years from now, you will always find yourself wondering what time can do. That no matter how many times you tell yourself that nothing is different, the world will always make you realize that a lot of things already changed.

Including every single person around you.

Even you.

"How do you view life?" she asked.

"I am not actually sure about it, but life's just full of random things, and I just pretend that most of them don't matter anyway." he answered.

"I see." She paused, smiled, and said,

"Totally opposite from mine, I guess."

Journey

And maybe the *most terrible,*

yet the *bravest thing* I've ever done

was to continue walking

no matter how *slow* my feet moved,

no matter how many times

I took a *rest* and sat on the ground—

to *stand up* and travel on this rocky road,

when all I ever wanted was

to *come back* to that wonderful moment

when things never seemed to be wrong,

when things never hurt so much,

and when everything seemed *perfectly fine.*

Dreams and Galaxies

I am *waiting* for something

that will never *happen.*

Yet,

someday I will be

the happiest—

and surprised

by something

I could never *imagine.*

That's when the *universe*

will show its *love for me.*

Favorite Stranger

Even if you find *someone new*

to talk to every night,

to hang out with every day,

to share with the giggles and laughter

on some corny jokes,

or to walk with and tell wonderful stories,

I'd still be here,

waiting for you to knock at my door

and sit beside me—

like we never missed each other.

I'd still be here,

even if you're with someone elsewhere.

I'd still be here,

patiently waiting and hoping.

I'd Love to Believe

Let's be strangers *again*.

Like we never knew each other.

As if we've never been *lovers*.

Think of me as someone who doesn't know you personally.

Spill out everything that hurts you. Tell me about your *heartbreaks* and all the things that *suffocate* you. I'll listen to all of the things you've done in the past, not caring if they will change my perspective or not.

Tell me how it hurts. As if you're talking to someone you think you'll never see again. As if you know your secrets will still be *safe* with me.

Let's go back to our beginnings.

Let's walk towards the start.

Let's be unknown to each other once more.

Maybe we will fall in love with each other after it all.

Halfway

I'd love to meet you elsewhere.

In a place where we wouldn't be both scared of accepting how we feel.

That we would understand how love isn't about *beautiful beginnings and happy endings.*

That most of the time, *it happens in between.*

Silence at a Distance

People can hurt you

without them laying

a *single* finger on you.

 People can make you cry

without them saying *any word*.

And that's what I've learned from

falling in love with you

when you already have someone else.

Behind the Naked Eyes

There's no such thing as love

at the first sight of *flaws*.

It's always the *good side*

you notice when you fall in love.

And I think that's what love does with you.

It lets you see the *beauty*

in everything and everyone.

Love Itself

You're the *rainbow* after the rain,

and the *sun* that rises in the morning.

You're one of the *constellations* at the night sky,

and the *dream* I've been wanting to have while I sleep.

You're beautiful for me

and if someone says otherwise,

always remember that someone believed you are.

Exit

I wish that falling in love

is just as *simple* as entering

and going out of someone's house—

that if I'm not entertained

so *sweetly and dearly,*

I can leave and never look back.

I wish that I can always find an *easy way out.*

But that's not how it is, and will never be.

Different Kind of Light

If you stare directly at the sun for *too long*,

it would make your eyes hurt.

Until you don't *notice*

that you're already crying.

One of my friends asked me

how I would feel if ever I see you

being *happy* with someone else.

And I said that's how it would feel.

Your smile would be *so bright*,

that I could no longer take it.

This is How I Miss You

I can't help but think of you every time it *rains*.

Your *memory* fills my thoughts

like the raindrops flooding the ground,

scattering everything that was already there.

And when it ends,

I'm left looking for the scattered pieces,

wondering how I could *fix* them.

Dangerously Closer

I've *built* a sand castle,

and you know what's *worse?*

I've built it near the shore,

where the waves can *wash* it

in just one single lap.

I've *met* you,

and you know what's *worse?*

I let myself be *closer* to you,

then I fell in love with you —

even if I know that in the end

it will only *crush* my heart into pieces.

I Should Never Regret Anything

I find myself thanking you

for all the *beautiful memories*

we've shared,

yet I still hope that instead of you,

I wish I could have *spent* those times

with someone else.

Someone who will never *leave.*

Someone who will *stay* forever.

Just like what you have once *promised.*

Stardust

You will always be something to me.

Something special.

Something I can't explain.

And when people come to me and ask who you are, I won't tell them everything I know. I want to keep you for myself. I'm selfless but when it comes to you, everything changes. I don't know how it happened.

I can't even look at you without falling in love all over again.

Like how I fell for you when I met you for the first time.

It's something extraordinary.

If I have a definition of magical, this is it.

It brings me to another world, where only the two of us know.

Back to One

And it is so hard to accept the *fact*

that we *risked* everything to love

and treat each other *more* than just a friend

but we suddenly became *strangers* again in the end.

It's Brighter on the Other Side

It is like a *pleasant dream*

when someone is very much willing

to love you,

no matter how *dark* you think

the way they need to pass through

just to get to *you.*

Not Going Anywhere

People say that

you'll realize the *worth*

of what you have

only when you *lose* it.

And that keeps me

thinking about you.

Did you just realize my worth

when you lost me?

Or you just forget everything

and the fact that *you still have me?*

Behind the Scenes

For the first time, *I totally see him.*

Not just how he looks.

Not just how he smiles.

I see him when he seems to be oblivious of his surroundings.

I see him when he's isolated from everyone.

I see him when he stays silent and doesn't say any single word. He gets my attention without even trying. He captures my eyes and leads them back to wherever he is.

I see him in a crowded room.

I see him in a loud noise.

I see him in a blurring hurricane.

I see him among the brightest stars.

I see him in a heavy traffic of slowly walking people.

I see him in a field of blooming flowers.

I see him in a dance floor full of swaying hips.

And I just realized how much I miss him.

How much I miss being the only girl he sees.

Sacrifices

And someday you'll realize

that some of the *reasons*

why you love that person

are not because of the *good things*

that they have done for you,

but because of the *bad things*

they will *never do* to hurt you.

Too Much Isn't Enough

But maybe you are

filling up the wrong box,

that doesn't *belong* with you.

Maybe you are *forcing*

to put the biggest sugar cube

inside the smallest bottle of wine,

that you ended up being *frustrated*

and walking away with a *broken heart*.

Confusion and Motivation

Then, she thought that love

was a *poison* that has no *antidote*,

but he made her realize that it was both.

Because love can either *kill* us

in a way that we'll refuse to move,

or it can make us feel *alive*

and sometimes with *hope*,

it pushes us to take another step forward.

Almost the End Game

He reminds me of a cold breeze during summer nights, when I refuse to fell asleep until midnight. He reminds me of a strange note I've found on my table when I'm about to go to work, saying good morning and wishing me a nice day.

He reminds me of sunsets with some drizzles.

He's the one I think of each and every time I see something beautiful, something wonderful that it makes my heart crave for more.

He's someone I haven't seen for a very long time now. But he will always be a book in my series.

A star in my constellation.

He's one of the best things that has ever happened to me.

And even if we hadn't ended up in each other's arms, he will always have that kiss and embrace that can make my heart feel warm.

Turning Reality

Someday, someone will hold my hand so *gentle,*

the one that can make me feel the *comfort.*

Someday, someone will look directly into my eyes,

and tell me the words I've been waiting to hear.

He will bring back the *stars in my sky,*

and bloom the *flowers in my garden* that had dried.

Someday, someone will never let me go,

and I'll be glad to stay with him *forever.*

A Beautiful Memory

In this world where time

continuously *goes on,*

some things will never change.

You'll always be that someone

that once made me *smile.*

You'll always be that person

that once brought *tears* into my eyes.

You're the scene where the *sun kisses the ocean,*

the one who once made me sad

and happy at the same time.

New Year's Eve

And all the sparks were *gone,*

like *fading* fireworks in the night sky.

All it has left were the echoes

of its booming sound

and a burnt stick falling right to the ground.

Our *memories* were loud enough

to drown the silence that surrounds.

Unexpected Turn

I have to admit that

some things will never be the same

without you.

Some songs will sound *different,*

some food will *no longer* taste as it used to do,

some days will be *colder,*

some places will look *darker.*

A lot of things might have changed

because of you,

but probably,

I might learn to love myself too.

Unsolved Mystery

Look at all the things

that love can do with people —

losing sleep, caring too much,

changing, growing, and happiness,

but where do all the loneliness

and pain come from?

Is it from the love

they never received in return?

I remember someone told me,

"Love won't always come back to you

from the same person you give love to."

I Wish I Could Hate You

I hate the sky.

I hate the moon.

I hate the sun.

I hate the stars.

I hate galaxies.

I hate the ocean.

I hate music.

I hate rainbows.

I hate sunset vibes.

I hate midnights.

I hate everything that reminds me of you.

I hate lying but hell, I just did.

Falling in Love

What if that someone doesn't have

the *intention* of breaking your heart?

What if that someone is *extremely worried*

to touch your heart,

that suddenly it had slipped from their hands

and come rolling onto the floor

and shattered into tiny pieces?

What if it's just doesn't *perfectly fit*

for them to hold?

But remember that there will be someone

who will hold on to you,

no matter what happens.

Walking the Other Way

Sometimes you're so *tired,*

that you choose

not to *break* any bridges.

Instead,

you turn around

and try to find a *different way,*

just to forget the past

finally,

without even looking back.

A Different Kind of Game

We used to play hide and seek *when we were kids,*

searching for a darker spot behind the trees

or somewhere in an abandoned house,

hoping the seeker won't see us,

waiting for our time to escape its tantalizing eyes.

And when you're the only one who was left hiding,

the others will stay quiet

even if they know where you are.

The seeker will just keep on exploring the place,

while you're doing your best to hide.

We used to play hide and seek when we were kids,

and somewhere deep inside your heart

there is still a little kid hiding—

hoping to be found.

Burning

You can stare at an art in a museum for too long,

but you're not allowed to bring it home.

You can look at the stars scattering in the night sky,

but you cannot reach them,

even if you have a pair of wings and fly.

You can hear and feel a soothing music,

but you cannot hold it with your hands.

There are things which were made just for you to admire,

those which were supposed to set a different kind of fire,

the one you should just stare and love from afar,

the one you shouldn't touch just to heal a single scar.

Maybe it can be the only thing you want to mend your heart,

but knowing you can't have it with you

can tear your world apart.

Eternity

I love you —

Until the sun stops rising and setting.

Until the stars lose their glow

Until the moon has its edges and becomes square.

Until the trees and flowers and fruits stop on growing.

Until the last bit of this universe

vanishes and crumbles into dust.

I love you, even if my heart stops on beating.

I love you —

Even if each and everything comes to its end.

YES!!! I just gave birth to my second baby,

"If Words Could Hold You."

I can't believe I just finished and published another book! It was exhausting and, of course, exciting at the same time. And for this second book, I would like to thank my proofreader, **Harold Patrick Mercado**, for doing the job for me. Also, for **Jehan Landong,** who provided amazing and beautifully made line arts for some of my writing. Usually, given that I am a self-published author, I would do all the work. But I honestly know that's not how it should be. That's why I searched for people who could help me make this happen. I extend my utmost gratitude for these amazing people.

I admit that my second book doesn't have any kind of story pattern, unlike my debut, **"When Things Are Not Fine."** I made this with a different theme and approach. I hope that this book was able to take you on a roller coaster of emotions. If not, please read it again. Kidding aside, I will still make and write pieces to widen my reach and keep communicating with my readers through words.

Once someone asked me, *"Why do you call your followers like*

"Sweetie"?" and I answered, **"Because I want to."**

It's the same answer I will give if someone asks me why I keep making books even if I am not sure if they will sell well. It's because I want to. Sometimes you just have to do it, without even an elaborate reason at all, especially if it makes your soul feel alive. *We have to take care of our souls, too.* I guess.

Whatever you're thinking, you're right. I make books not only for my readers but also for my own satisfaction. I make books so that I can see wherever this experience will lead me.

I take risks because I want to grow as a human being and become the best version of myself. I will continue to make mistakes, but I will always remember to learn from them.

I know that not all of us have the same circumstances. And I won't push anyone to take on the same risks. But please know that if there's something that makes your soul feel alive, you have to do it, even just once. And if there's none, you'll have to wait and look for it somewhere else. Maybe it's not where you are now. But one day, I genuinely hope that you encounter it in this life.

Thank you so much for always being here with me.

We're still staring at the same sky, aren't we?

I am so glad that you exist.

Please take care of yourself,

and may you receive everything that you need.

If you keep on working for what your soul desires,

I hope the universe will help you reach it.

It is always a pleasure to write for you again and again.

MA.C.A

If you want to reach me personally, please never hesitate to send a message to any of my social accounts:

E-mail address: vomitingwords11@gmail.com

Facebook: vmtngwords

Instagram: iamvomitingwords

Tiktok: vmtngwords

Tumblr: vomitingwords

If you want to work with Mr. Harold Patrick Mercado, you can look him up on Facebook, and you can also check out some of his books.

Same goes for Ms. Jehan Landong, you can look her up on Facebook, and you can also see some of her amazing artwork.

THAN YOU EVERYONE,

FOR YOUR NEVER ENDING SUPPORT!!!